1

G000135872

The Words of the Wise Old Paratrooper by Robin Horsfall.

Edited by Oliver Horsfall

www.robinhorsfall.co.uk

© 2017 Robin Horsfall

o.horsfall@gmail.com

Cover by Ernie McGookin.

ISBN: 978-1-973-299-813

THE WORDS OF THE WISE OLD PARATROOPER

ROBIN HORSFALL

TO ALL MY DEPARTED COMRADES.

NEVER FORGOTTEN.

The Author

Robin Horsfall was a soldier from the age of fifteen up to the age of

thirty-two. He served with the Parachute Regiment, the SAS, The

Sultans of Oman's Armed Forces, The Army of Sri Lanka and was a

Major in 'Frelimo' The Army of Mozambique. He studied Karate for

[1] Photo. Heather Horsfall

most of his adult life achieving the rank of 6th Dan Black Belt until in 2011 a neck fracture halted his career. During his recovery he went to Surrey University and studied English literature and creative writing graduating in 2016. Married since 1981 this father of five and grandfather of ten started posting *'The Sayings of the Wise Old Paratrooper'* on Facebook and later decided to collate them along with his short stories and poetry into this collection.

Background

At the age of twenty-three or thereabouts I was an isolated and

rather cynical young soldier struggling to find a place in life. I had

recently taken up the art of karate and came across an article in

Combat magazine in which there was a short saying which had a

profound effect on my future. It read 'When in company never discuss the faults of others and when alone contemplate your own thoughts.' I cut the piece out and pasted it to the sloping ceiling above my bed. Those few words carried an important lesson that changed my life for the better.

I discovered as the years passed that my true vocation in life was teaching; it didn't matter what I taught I just loved the thrill of imparting information to others especially children. There was a joy in seeing their confidence and abilities grow in response to my work. During classes, I often found myself using short metaphorical sayings. Sometimes they were humorous and at other times thought provoking - occasionally they were a path to force someone to be introspective. Such sayings are an old method of teaching and they can carry great weight. I know that wiser and older people have voiced the same thoughts in similar words and where I can locate that individual I give them credit but when I quote the 'Wise Old

Paratrooper', I am to the best of my knowledge using my own thoughts and words.

I was inspired by the war poems of Siegfried Sassoon, Wilfred Brooks, Rudyard Kipling and also the songs of Barry Sadler and Harvey Andrews.

I broke my neck when I was fifty-four when I was a full time karate instructor. As I recovered I applied for a degree course at Surrey University studying English Literature with Creative Writing. The different poetic forms were fascinating and fun. I have tried to use a variety of these to express my feelings and I have also introduced a series of short, light hearted military stories to balance some of the deep and sad philosophical aspects of this collection. It is important to remember our sad losses but just as important to recall the laughs, the fun and the joy of life too.

Inspiration

*

Wrote a poem today

Never wrote before

Never wrote anything

I'll never write amore.

***

'A wise man will put into words what you

already know.'

Growing up

*

**'Whether you start from the top or the bottom in life you can
stand still or move in one direction.'**

'If there's something about you that you can't understand, something

that makes you unpopular with your peers then you will develop a personality that is independent. Your isolation from friends will impose this characteristic upon you. That independence might be perceived as arrogance or petulance - it is neither. It is a protection, a defence against unkindness created by distrust and it is also a defence against loneliness. You will learn to manage without the help or the generosity of others. You will ask no favours and unwittingly perpetuate the isolation that you desperately hope will end. Others will watch and wait for you to fail. If you stagger they will say 'I knew he would get his comeuppance in the end'. If you don't fail and instead succeed they will resent you for proving them wrong.'

***

- 'Smile, speak clearly and listen.'
- 'You can't reduce an opponent's abilities, you can only increase your own.'
- 'Put brain into gear before putting mouth into motion.'
- 'If your body consumes trash you will have a trash body. If your brain consumes trash......'.

- 'Stupid is as stupid does.'

- 'Discover what you are good at and then be the best.'

- 'There are no bad schools just bad teachers.'

- Every human brain is phenomenal it has unlimited potential - so use it!'

- 'New apples won't improve a rotten barrel.'

- 'When someone is caught lying the first response is denial, the second aggression, the third is bartering and then a return to the start. Acceptance only comes when the first three fail.'

- 'You can't take back your actions - you can only ensure you don't repeat them.'

- 'Take responsibility for your mistakes.'

'Lots of bad boys grow up to be good men.'

- 'The first great shock in life in discovering that your parents aren't perfect. The second is discovering that neither are you!'

- 'I pick on you most because you are the only one who is worth the effort.'

- ''Don't learn the hard way - learn the right way!'

Pantoum Of The Mountains

Ice created rock and stream

Distant views of ancient shores

Heights that recall youthful dreams

Heather's coat with crimson horns

Distant views of ancient shores

Travelled climbed with fainting stress

Heather's coat with crimson horns

Sheltered in a cave's egress

Travelled climbed with fainting stress

Torn and bruised on soaring towers

Sheltered in a cave's egress

Broke my heart's enormous powers

Worn and bruised on soaring towers

Frozen shaking weakened boy

Broke my heart's enormous powers

Saw a fool a trembling toy

Frozen shaking weakened boy

Ice created rocks and streams

Saw a fool a trembling toy

Heights that recall youthful dreams.

**'It's not the gifts you are born with that make you special - it's
how you use them.'**

- 'Never use the 'C' word. "Can't" should never enter into your vocabulary'.

- 'Sing your knowledge and dance the joy of learning.'

- 'There is darkness in us all - if we don't accept that truth then there is nothing we can do about it'.

- 'Accept responsibility for the consequences of your actions.

- 'Sticks and stones will break your bones but cruel names will break your heart.'

- 'The less you speak about yourself the more others will speak about you.'

- 'In the battle between hormones and common sense hormones always wins.'

- 'Wanna be tough? Go to school, feed your kids and love your wife!'

- 'In the land of the blind the one eyed man is a threat.'

- 'Don't run yourself down there are plenty of volunteers who will do that for you!'

John

In 1980 after B Squadron had successfully assaulted the Iranian

Embassy in London we were loaded into the back of a large, yellow

truck and whisked away to Regents Park Barracks to organise our

gear and return to Hereford. We were still the Counter Terrorist

Team and we had to be ready for another call out.

When we arrived we were informed that Prime Minister Margaret

Thatcher would be coming to see us to say thank you. She arrived a

short time later with her husband Dennis and after a few moments we lined up to shake hands with the 'Iron Lady'. She was small and I noticed her thick make up as she laid her hand in mine. I was twenty-three years old and impressed.

A television had been placed in the corner of the large, unfurnished room so that we could watch the events that we had taken part in a couple of hours before. As we gathered for the news report Maggie stood in the front.

The BBC news report came on and we heard the music while the presenter made his announcements. We pushed and jostled for a view of the television but Maggie's head and hair were causing a considerable obstruction to the view of at least one member of our team. John's Glaswegian voice boomed from the back of the room 'Hey hun could ya git yer f***ing heed oot of the wee? I canna see the telly.'

Some of us laughed and others grimaced but Maggie turned and said 'Oh sorry of course' and stepped to one side.

- 'Question authority, don't blindly obey it'.

- 'You've got to get it wrong before you get it right'

- 'Only drink in good company'.

- 'If you reward a dog when it whines guess what it will do?'

- 'There's nothing like doing nothing to make you feel like doing nothing.'

- 'Sarcasm kills curiosity!'

- 'If it never rains but always pours there is one cause.'

- 'Nothing comes to he who sits on his arse and waits.'

- 'I you don't 'know your place' by the time you are twenty-five you are probably on the path to success.

- 'We are all the sum of our own decisions.'

- 'It's hard to be objective about an individual who is being judgemental.'

- 'Burn all your bridges there is no going back!'

- 'When people get deeply entrenched in their beliefs on opposing sides they can not or will not stop hating.'

Fighting

'Bullying is a common form of human behaviour founded in the desire to dominate another individual. If you isolate, humiliate or intimidate another person you are without qualification ... a bully!'

- 'Tolerance is not for the appeasement of the intolerant.'

- 'If you carry a knife you will end up dead or in prison.'

---

[2] Photo. Richard Goulding.

- 'To win a fight, stop worrying about your enemy - make your enemy worry about you'.

- 'I didn't teach students martial arts to defeat martial artists - I taught them martial arts to defeat idiots!'

- 'If a man behaves like a donkey treat him like an ass.' (Shigeru Kimura)

- 'If you are fighting a lion be a fox'.

- 'To obtain victory focus all your thoughts and actions towards a single objective.'

- 'Threats are not actions, in most cases they are bluster.'

- 'Prepare for the worst so that any other result is a bonus.'

- 'An angry man is a foolish man.'

- 'One good punch might save a thousand words but it could cost a million'.

- 'It's not what you do but what you say that convicts you.'

- 'Killing people is easy. Not killing when there's a gun in your hand … that's hard to do.'

- 'You cannot defeat belief with logic'.

- 'You can't explain a colour to a blind man.'

- 'Like attracts like.'

- 'Don't ask a thirsty man to carry your water.'

- 'Cowards will always judge your courage'.

- 'You are only as good as your last day's training.'

- 'Call those punches? I can kiss harder than that. Ask your wife!' (Encouraging a karate class).

- 'Tough guys are like onions when you peel back the layers there is nothing left except tears'.

- 'When you get past fifty a fight should be over before your assailant knows it has started.'

- 'Volunteers make the best students.'

'It isn't a question of can you fight? It's a question of will you?

Soldiering

'We should not be ashamed of defeating our enemies.'

- 'Only drink in good company'.

- 'Keep your powder dry.'

- 'You can defeat an idea with firepower but you need an endless supply of ammunition'.

- 'Talk is cheap it is also very easy'.

- 'Shock horror!! Latest discovery by journalists 'Soldiers issued with guns and ammunition kill people in wars'.

- 'You can't train men to be tigers by day and pussycats by night!'

- 'Winning isn't the same as victory and losing isn't necessarily defeat.'

- 'Freedom has to be fought for. There is no such thing as a free, pacifist society.'

- 'Don't get soft shoes, get hard feet!'

- 'Kill the terrorists - save the hostages. Not too complicated really.'

- 'Don't get your ambitions confused with your abilities.'

- 'Never argue with corporal when zipped up in sleeping bag.'

'War is more mud than blood'.

'Don't mess with the SAS – or their wives!'

Jok

In 1975 the 2nd Battalion the Parachute Regiment was approximately

fifty percent Scottish - Jok was one of those fifty percent. Short,

fierce and extremely proud he would fight anyone for any reason.

When he was in a violent mood he was best left alone but in contrast

he had a dry and wicked humour.

It was October and the battalion was 'dug in' on Salisbury Plain. The trenches that the men had dug in the red soil gradually filled with water and mud. Soaking wet men shivered and swore as nightfall came. The sides of trenches collapsed and we were forced to rebuild them or risk punishment for leaving our watery holes to sit on the ground alongside. There was little point in making such improvements as it would only be a matter of hours before the company moved and a new position would have to be dug again. As night came our position became silent the only sound was the intermittent hiss of the radio. Occasionally a radio check would be called in by the Company Commander - Sunray Charley.

Jok was our platoon signaller and he was huddles beneath a plastic poncho at the bottom his trench with his ear phones over one ear. A voice message came in.

'Hello Charlie one this is Sunray Charley, radio check over.'

Jok took his frozen hands from between his legs and pressed the radio switch.

'Okay over'

The reply came back 'Okay out'.

'Prat' he said to himself - referring indirectly to Sunray .

An hour passed and we all tried to sleep as the rain poured though the gaps in our clothing and soaked us to the skin. Jok pressed the radio switch and said for all to hear,

'I'm fucking pissed off'.

There was a long hiss of static and then a reply.

'Hello unknown call sign this is Sunray Charley– send call sign over.'

There was a short pause before Jok replied.

'I'm not that fucking pissed off!'

Sound Over Battle

There's a sound hangs over battle

When the fight is done and won

There's a sound hangs over battle

That can't be made a song

There's a sound hangs over battle

In both vict'ry and defeat

It makes no bloody difference

It's bitter never sweet!

The singing of the mountains and the rain upon my face

The fading light of evening marks a place of holy grace

Of ground that holds our men and boys who followed in the chase

To sons, and brothers, friends and foes who lost the violent race.

There's a sound hangs over battle

When the ground's no longer red

There's a sound hangs over battle

Unheard by those abed.

There's a sound hangs over battle

That few men would want to share

There's a sound hangs over battle

It's heard by those who dare.

The singing of the mountains and the rain upon my face

The fading light of evening marks a place of holy grace

Of ground that holds our men and boys who followed in the chase

To sons, and brothers, friends and foes who lost the violent race.

There's a sound hangs over battle

The crows and vultures know

There's a sound hangs over battle

Where no caw nor bark can grow.

There's a sound hangs over battle

That few will ever hear

There's a sound hangs over battle

Called the silence after fear

The singing of the mountains and the rain upon my face

The fading light of evening marks a place of holy grace

Of ground that holds our men and boys who followed in the chase

To sons, and brothers, friends and foes who lost the violent race.

***

- 'An action isn't right because everyone else does it!'

- 'Being a special soldier doesn't make you a special person.'

- 'Soldiers don't 'give their lives', they lose them.'

- 'It's not heroic to be murdered it's sad. It's not heroic to provide help to the injured it's expected. It's not heroic to fight an illness when you have no other choice. It is heroic to voluntarily place yourself into a lethal situation to defeat evil and support your brothers in arms.'

- 'The modern soldier has a choice; Kill the enemy and be arrested or be killed by the enemy'

- 'Incoming artillery can cause an epiphany.'

- 'There is no soldier as fierce, courageous and knowledgeable as a keyboard warrior.'

- 'Listen, read, absorb, think,- think again then comment.'

Old Friend

Is it wrong that I should weep

To say goodbye my friend?

Should I stand firm and hold my grief

And still a quivering lip?

Right to stand among the strong

Display my manly power

38

And watch the passing of your life

Without a tearful shower?

Should I burst and sob and cry

Reveal my sense of loss

And let the world see how it is

To show a brother's love?

Or will I cause *real men* to blush

And raise their signs to hush?

***

- 'I can handle stupidity and I can handle aggression. I can't stand stupid aggression.'

- 'It's better to be the idiot in charge than the idiot being told what to do'.

- 'Grunts have the ability to smell bullshit at a thousand yards.'

War

Should I go or should I stay

I could always run away

Am I a man or a boy

Or just a general's toy?

Sir Galahad

Grey ships

Grey seas

Grey skies

Blue skies

Red ships

Red seas.

Hector

It wouldn't have created much argument if in 1980 someone had described Hector as 'difficult'. In the three years that I served under him I don't recall that he ever smiled or laughed. He had a fixed moral compass which only read 'My Way'. Other adjectives were just as appropriate, grim, gruff, dynamic, aggressive, demanding, intolerant and just plain nasty. His most redeeming features were that he could lead his men and motivate them to fight. This meant that he was only useful in one context – battle. If he didn't have a reason to fight he would find or make one.

He kept a little black book and recorded every incident that ever occurred with any soldier under his command. In 1981 during an 'interview' he took out his book and reminded me of a mistake I had made six years previously as a young eighteen year old private soldier. He had many nicknames the kindest of which were 'Hector the Director' and 'The Whirling Smock'.

He planned and led Operation Nimrod the famous SAS assault on the Iranian Embassy in London 1980 and he prepared us for Operation Mikado a suicide mission into Argentina during the Falklands War of 1982. Positive aggressive and determined he never let us believe in anything but complete success but he ruled with fear. Fear of being returned to unit and fear of being a failure. He rarely gave second chances.

On the 22nd December 1979 I joined his Sabre Squadron in Northern Ireland. In my first week as a member of the squadron I watched the unit do nothing except get drunk over Christmas. On 3rd January 1980 Hector arrived for an inspection and asked me how I liked life with the squadron. I told him that it was hard to say as most of them had been pissed since I arrived, he wasn't impressed. Over the next few years those accurate and honest remarks were never forgotten. Honesty I learned was not the best policy especially for a new boy.

In 1982 I was part of a medical operation in Oman. The Omani desert in summer is a tough place to live, plagued by sand, flies and diarrhoea the temperatures were often in excess of 45C. When the wind blew it was like a hot hairdryer. Exposed skin burned and cracked and food was amply mixed with sand. There was little to do except work and survive.

We had been working hard under these conditions for more than a month when Hector arrived on a helicopter for a brief visit. He wandered over to where I was preparing my medical equipment for the next foray into the empty wilderness. I saw him coming but concentrated on my equipment hoping that he would pass me by but I heard his footsteps halt just behind me, 'I hear you have done well'. The hackles sat up on my neck in warning. 'What do think of this place?' I looked down at the ground, took a breath and said 'It's f***ing great Boss, f***ing great! I love it here.'

'If you don't like the truth people will tell you what you want to hear.'

***

- 'A loose cannon destroys the ship that it is supposed to protect. A loose mouth can do the same.'

- 'When you attack my people I become your terrorist.'

- 'Bullshit baffles brains.'

- 'Crazy people make you crazy.'

- 'I can't count what I used to have, what I might have, or what others have. I can only count what I have now and for the moment be content.'

Engerland

Find a nice woman in a good town,

Start a small business, settle down,

Get a parking fine, tear up the ticket

Without realising it's a sticky wicket.

Go to court and get found guilty,

Watch the account go soft and wilty.

Get the Focus towed away,

Ask for time to work and pay.

Try two jobs to make ends meet

And walk to work on blistered feet.

Ask and pray for a helping hand

From the Government of Engerland.

-

You must be joking!

Politics

'It's not what you say that's important. It's who's listening.'

- 'If you don't vote – don't bitch.'

- 'First take fifty bored kids, add a little history and stir well with several large spoonsful of hate. Serve slowly and distribute to each individual with a £10 note for seasoning.' (Recipe for an Irish Republican demonstration).

- 'It's hard to be an eagle when you're surrounded by tits.'

---

5 Photo Mark Leishman

- 'A foul odour emanates from these letters. It is the same foul odour that emanates from this house. It is the smell of fear, the smell of cowardice, it is the smell of betrayal!' (At Westminster Feb 2017. Justice for Northern Ireland Veterans.)

- 'Adolf Hitler was democratically elected'.

- 'Walls keep people in as well as out'. (Trump's wall 2017)

- 'Fame by association makes everyone special.'

- 'Argument from ignorance includes 'I heard, I saw, I read, I knew a bloke who, a person I respect said and I believe? To make a point use verifiable, objective evidence.'

21st Century Soldier

'If you want to join the army

If you want to go to war

If you want to be a soldier

Get locked up when you get older

If you want to go to prison

Go to war!'

49

***

- 'When fools vote the winner is the biggest fool.' (Election of Donald Trump)

- 'Be careful what you wish for'. (In response to being asked to become an MP.)

- 'The best way to end a war is with a winner.'

- 'Don't tell your leaders what they ought to do - go out and do it yourself!'

- 'It's so frustrating knowing all the answers - if only they would just put *you* in charge?'

- 'The better you know foreign people the harder it is to hate them.'

- 'Fear creates enemies, fear creates wars, fear demands obedience. There is nothing more desirable to some leaders than obedience.'

Neil

Nasty Neil was a 'Booty', he had transferred from the Royal Marines

to the SAS in the early 1970's. Dour and dry humoured Neil was

highly respected as a soldier's soldier. He once ran forty miles across

the desert with two water bottles a rifle and a compass to get help

for a patrol whose vehicle was bogged down in wet sand.

During one exercise in Oman we had been working as a small team

for a long time and were due a break. This 'break' consisted of a

helicopter flying in a resupply that included fresh meat and vegetables and a ration of G10 rum. The plan was to barbeque the

meat and mix the rum with our tea. However, by coincidence the

very same day a team of hydrographers discovered our outpost and

asked to share the evening with us. Their leader was a Major in the

Omani Southern Defence Force. When Neil discovered that they had

a few crates of cold beer in their truck he happily agreed to the

suggestion and offered the Major his camp bed and tent for the

night.

By midnight the rum and beer had produced a predictable result and

Neil wandered up to me with a pick helm in his hand. His eyes had a

threatening look but when I asked him what his intentions were he

faltered and wandered away slightly confused. I thought no more

about it until early the next morning when the Major and his team

were preparing to depart. Neil was nowhere to be seen but loud

snores from his tent were enough to explain why. The Major was

laughing and told us the reason for his humour. Neil having forgotten his promise had appeared with his pick helm still in hand at his tent in the middle of the night demanding his bed back. Wisdom prevailed over promises and the Major retreated to his vehicle without resistance. He asked us to thank Neil for his hospitality and drove off with a cheery wave. We left Neil to sleep off the booze.

The plan for the day was to direct Hawker Hunter jets in low level practise attacks on selected targets in the desert - I was the Forward Air Controller.

The jet established communications and I directed it onto my first selected target - Neil's tent. As the jet roared in I shouted 'SAM-SAM-SAM' into the radio. The message indicated to the pilot that a surface to air missile had been launched against him. The pilot fired his afterburners and climbed as fast as he could into the sky - the

roar was tremendous and the sides of Neil's tent fluttered upwards in a futile attempt to follow the aircraft.

A face with a pair of sad bloodshot eyes protruded from the entrance as Neil said good morning to the world. We spent the remainder of the day persuading him that he had assaulted the Major with the pick handle and that he had gone off in a very bad mood. His vague recollection was enough to convince him that there was some truth in our story. 'Oh no' he exclaimed 'Another nail in the coffin of my career'. It was only at the end of a long hot day that we let him off the hook and told him the truth.

Everything in this story does bear a resemblance to persons who lived their lives to the full!

***

- 'The USA is always the best of friends - with the USA.'

- 'Don't invite a tiger to share your steak lunch and think that the tiger will appreciate your kindness.' (Negotiations with terrorists).

- 'People love you when you tell them what they want to hear'.

- 'The good thing about democracy is that when there is a huge undercurrent of popular feeling or resentment it has the opportunity to vent itself without revolution.'

- 'Well folks - that's democracy'. (President Trump's election).

- 'Only a fool would argue with a pig.'

- 'One day my enemy's enemy will be my enemy too.'

- 'The IRA never released any prisoners.'

- 'Referendums are like medals sometimes they are meaningless.' (Brexit)

- 'It is the responsibility of the press to report the news responsibly'.

- 'The greatest barrier to positive change is the apathy of the public.'

- 'When you resurrect the dead you resurrect their problems.'

- 'It will all be different when I'm in charge!!!'

Honour & Integrity

'It lowers a man to dance on someone's grave.' Few of us regret seeing the life of a tyrant, terrorist or murderer come to an end but it avails us nought to revel in their deaths. Such behaviour lowers us to the level of the mob and those who support such people. They will answer to their gods and in their last moments that possibility will pass through their minds. They will die frightened of the unknown as all evil men and women do.' (On the death of IRA Commander Martin Mcguiness).

- 'Honour is living by someone else's standards. Integrity is striving to live according to your own'.

- 'If you want to be admired behave admirably.'

- 'Don't be surprised if betrayal kicks you in the arse one day.'

- 'Always give a fool the last word.'

- 'When a man disagrees with you it doesn't make him your enemy.'

- 'If you say "Yes" and then change your mind you are a villain. If you say "No" and then change your mind you are a hero.'

- 'Never believe your own press.'

- 'Manners make the civilised man'

- 'Don't do something by day that you can't sleep with at night'.

- 'Don't do what is expedient, do what is right.'

- 'It's the message not the author that's important.'

- 'The only place to insult someone is alone and to their face'.

- 'A man who has become too important for his old friends will struggle to make new ones'.

- 'Rank or title should imply honesty or integrity - but it doesn't.'

- 'An argument is never enhanced by vulgar language'.

- 'Good men can do very bad things and some bad men love their kids'.

- 'Form your opinions of people on what you see or know - not on what you hear.'

- 'If you want to help someone, carry their load - don't weigh them down with good advice.'

- 'When people are slating an absent friend or enemy ask them to talk about someone they like.'

- 'Money is only a tool; friends are real assets'.

- 'Sometimes silence is the best reply'.

- 'The eventual punishment for wickedness is loneliness'.

- 'Everyone else knows what you shouldn't do and what you should have done'.

- 'Don't arm your enemy's enemies'.

- 'You cannot be responsible for other people's bad behaviour.'

- 'We shouldn't be comfortable believing bad things about people we dislike.'

- 'If you have nothing good to say - say nothing.'

Charles

Charles was tall, blue eyed and according to most women

extraordinarily handsome. I had known him since I was eighteen - he

was two years older than me and already one of the Parachute

Regiment's elite free fall team The Red Devils.. When he wasn't

performing as a 'Sky God' he would return to normal duties as a

member of 2 Para Mortar Platoon.

One night at about midnight the door creaked open and Charles sneaked into our four-man room with a young woman on his arm. Although the lights stayed off and we remained silent it was difficult not to be aware of what was taking place across the room.

A few whispered words were followed by an exclamation from Charles. 'Okay, I can arrange that!'

The lights went on and Charles leapt up and drew a large bag from beneath his bed.

'Get up you lot' he shouted this lady is going parachuting.'

Intrigued and interested we watched and assisted Charles to fit the naked girl into the harness of his freefall parachute and white helmet with a red devil emblazoned on the side. The webbing did little for her modesty but it was all in fun. Charles pulled the rip-cord and spilled the chute onto the floor and then opened the window – we were two floors above the ground about thirty feet high. Initially we were worried that he intended to drop her to the ground but it soon became clear that his intention was to lower her to the floor by gently feeding her out the window on the rigging lines.

The large square window was conveniently tipped back to the horizontal and we sat her on the ledge trying hard to avoid injury on the window latch. We lowered the 'latest Red Devil' to the ground to shouts of glee 'I'm a paratrooper' she shouted.

As four heads leaned out of the window to watch her descent a shadow in uniform appeared in the dark. Six feet from the ground we dropped her onto the gravel where she sat half covered by parachute silk. 'I'm a paratrooper! I'm a paratrooper!' she shouted.

The shadow loomed over her silhouetted against the night sky and spoke - 'I'm very glad you've landed safely madam and I'm glad you're a paratrooper. I'm the duty officer and I think it's time you rolled up your parachute and went home.'

Success

'Never let others tell you what you can't achieve!

- 'There are no bad schools only bad teachers!'

- 'Never start a response with 'Yes, but…'

- 'Never ask a question you don't want to hear the answer to.'

- 'Don't put yourself down - there are plenty of volunteers who will do that for you.'

- Don't let pushy people use your good nature against you.'

- 'Stop bloody whining'.

- 'Shit happens... especially if you choose to swim in it.'

- 'Do one thing well - not many things badly'.

- 'High achievers start by doing what others won't do and finish by doing what others can't do'.

- 'A man who constantly looks backwards will make little progress'.

- 'Don't get too deep in a muddy pond.'
- 'Don't tell me what you think. Tell me what you can do'.

- 'Wanna job? Tell me how you can make me or save me money!'

- 'History doesn't remember those who weren't there'.

- 'If something needs doing do it now!'

- 'A bad tool man blames his works'.

- 'To be special you don't have to do extraordinary things you only have to do ordinary things extraordinarily well.'

- There's can do people and might do people, I know which ones I prefer.'

- 'Don't do half a job.'

- 'Always volunteer.'

- 'Own your things. Don't let your things own you'.

- 'There's nothing like doing nothing to make you feel like doing nothing.'

- 'Victory and success are opposite sides of the same coin.'

- 'If you live your life as a tragedy it will become one.'

- 'One of the problems of writing innuendo is that so few are capable of reading between the lines. There we are then!'

- 'The safer the car the faster the driver.'

- 'Choking is thinking too slow, panicking is thinking too fast.'

- 'There is a huge difference between an explanation and an excuse.'

Illusion

I've done it - I'm in

The best there's ever been

The soldiers who we test

Always tougher than the rest.

Hooray, here I am

Make us work, make us plan

Give us jobs, give us courses

Make us work like horses.

What no jobs, no orders?

No patrolling over borders?

Just rush then wait.

Were you at Prince's gate?

Ireland, hah! - Where's that?

No soldiers went on that.

The action wasn't even warm

Unless you went on Storm

Tough guys from the past

Bloody heroes to the last.

Millions of dead

Killed by sheets of lead.

Don't do any training

Especially when it's raining

Just lie and cheat -

Pretend to be elite!

***

- 'Form your opinions of people on what you see not on what you hear.'

- 'Don't shout at the enemy when your friends are stabbing you in the back.'

Laughter & Tears

'Sometimes you just have to stop being serious and laugh'.

- 'The most wonderful thing about going fishing online is when you get a byte.'

- 'It's only a game ..... especially when your team loses.

- 'The world is full of dyslexic bankers'.

- 'Isn't it nice to think that you are the only one who is incorruptible'.

- 'No pain no brain.'

- 'Block everyone who sends you a chain letter.'

- 'If space-time is infinite then everything that is possible must eventually happen.' (Intellectual moment).

- 'A son is a son 'till he takes him a wife but a daughter's a daughter for all of your life!'

- 'In 2016 more people died of obesity than died in war and crime combined. Be afraid - be very afraid - of sugar!'

- 'We spend most of our lives in a neutral state, not happy or sad - just somewhere in between.'

Minky

December 1979 found B squadron 22 SAS in Portadown, Northern

Ireland. The winter weather was typically Irish, cold with endless rain.

After Christmas had passed, operations seemed to wither away as

the IRA and UDA remained at home to play with their new train sets.

In consequence the squadron's reaction was to do the same. As a

new boy and never much of a drinker I watched as the world's most

professional soldiers drank until they dropped. When New Year's Eve

arrived even the most hardened consumers of alcohol were slowing

down - except Minky.

Minky was a Royal Engineer with the constitution of an Ox. What he drank could have and would have killed most men. He could remain standing hour after hour drink after drink until lesser mortals succumbed to sleep.

Soldiers who have over imbibed will recall that no matter how drunk they were and how far from home - their sozzled brains would automatically make a plan for the legs to walk them home to bed. Those who failed would end up in flower-beds or doorways in a pool of regurgitated food.

Minky was an expert, his legs always got him to his bed. The prospect of failure on a cold Northern Irish night could have been fatal.

It was New year's day 1980 at about 0300. A few of us observed as Minky staggered from the bar and we watched as his autopilot (to bed) switched on: open the bar door –turn right – bounce along the wall as far as the corner and turn right again. Fifty long strides across the tarmac to the end of the third porta-cabin, grab the bannister by the foot of the steps and throw up. Pause, wipe face then climb the five steps – push handle down and enter. Slide left shoulder along wall as far as the third door on the left. Open door - walk towards left corner of room and collapse on bed.

The autopilot worked perfectly until the very last moment when Minky fell and curled up on the floor to sleep ... The boys had stolen his bed!

***

The Law

- 'Don't get justice confused with the law'.
- 'The rule of law only works when the law has the support of the people'. (Causes of terrorism).
- It's not what you do, it's what you say that convicts you.' (Self –defence).

- 'The law is not about finding the truth. The law is about finding the best argument!'

***

The Spirit of Remembrance

I watched you marching past today,

November light your hair showed grey

Children called as they ran alongside,

I saw the pride in your wife's brown eyes.

The years are long and the ground is cold,

I watch you march with the old and bold,

Remember me, remember me.

Do you remember me?

You're happy now as you march on by.

You promised to return I saw the lie.

You loved me then, do you love me now?

True brothers bound in blood and war

The years are long and the ground is cold,

I watch you march with the old and bold,

Remember me, remember me.

Do you remember me?

You held me tight - the blood still flowed,

I died you left me by the road.

Our medals worn with pride attest,

To heroes who fought with the best.

The years are long and the ground is cold,

I watch you march with the old and bold,

Remember me, remember me.

Do you remember?

6

'November 11th is for Remembrance - the rest of the year is to enjoy your life'

---

[6] Photo. David Murphy.

Christmas

- 'It's Christmas Eve - fill yer boots.'

- 'This month spend as much as you can borrow, eat as much sweet and fattening food as you can, get drunk for a week or two, worry about debt, get angina, have a fight with a stranger in a pub, embarrass yourself at work, watch endless TV advertisements about war victims and starving children, listen to Slade singing 'So here it is Merry Christmas'. Drink *Gaviscon* every day, put up offensive remarks on Facebook about everyone who thinks you are an idiot and - have yourself a very merry Christmas time.' (December 2016).

- 'If you want to enjoy Christmas cut up your credit card, don't borrow money for stuff you can't afford and feel good about depriving the banks of your cash.'

- 'Christmas is over; now it's time to plan next year's battles.'

Departing

Little blossom made me smile

Now on winds you fly away

Dark clouds gather in my heart

Will I smile again?

Petals grow and bloom

Protect your sweet heart from cold

Falling tears follow your path

Will I smile again?

***

- 'It's better to have a bad friend than a terrible enemy.'

- 'It isn't the meek who will inherit the earth. It will be the hungry, the angry and the disenfranchised.'

- 'The worst parts of life sometimes create the best results.'

- 'Six billion flies *can* all be wrong.'

***

Suicide

There's a terrible sadness hangs over my soul

Where love held its court there's dead empty space

Where my heart used to be there's only a hole

I don't know the cause I've just lost my place

Frank

There's a terrible sadness hang over my soul

Have I done all I can, no more oats to sow?

Perhaps my life's done and I don't have a role

And now cos I'm old there is nowhere to go

Keith

There's a terrible sadness hangs over my soul

Will you manage without me after my show?

When the sun has gone down and night is like coal

Will this weight last forever? How will I know?

Nish

There's a terrible sadness hangs over my soul

Sometimes for no reason I'd wave life goodbye

I want to let go and hide far below

But I know I would miss tomorrow's blue sky.

Soldier's Song

On the desert road to Baghdad, did you care?

When the ground began to shake were you there?

With the dead along the streets little kids beneath old sheets

Was there time between your meets

In your chair? Did you care? Was it fair?

---

[7] Photo. Denzil Connick

82

I'm looking for a shadow hoping for a drink

Walking past an I. E.D and trying not to think

Fighting for a gen'ral a thousand miles away

Eating lousy rations while he tries to cut our pay

As I walked the Afghan plain, where were you?

Every night beneath the rain was nothing new.

In your nice warm bed at night did you waken with a fright

Did she make it all right and stroke your hair.

Did you care? Did you care? Did you care?

I'm looking for a shadow hoping for a drink

Walking past an I. E.D and trying not to think

Fighting for a gen'ral a thousand miles away

Eating lousy rations while he tries to cut our pay

When you lied and our wives cried, did you care?

Leaving love and life behind made men weep

When our homes had broken hearts and our pain was off the charts

When you sent us faulty parts

Were you there? Were you there? Were you there?

I'm looking for a shadow hoping for a drink

Walking past an I. E.D and trying not to think

Fighting for a gen'ral a thousand miles away

Eating lousy rations while he tries to cut our pay

When my wife said welcome home, were you there?

When she pushed me down the street a broken man.

When my pension was delayed

As my legs were being made

Was it fair? Was it fair? Was it fair?

I'm looking for a shadow hoping for a drink

Walking past an I. E.D and trying not to think

Fighting for a gen'ral a thousand miles away

Eating lousy rations while he tries to cut our pay

When the dreams come in the night will you dare

To share with me my wet and lonely shame

Will my medals help my slumber was I just an army number

Is it you we must remember?

Don't you care? Don't you bloody dare - Tony Blair.

I'm looking for a shadow hoping for a drink

Walking past an I. E.D and trying not to think

Fighting for a gen'ral a thousand miles away

Eating lousy rations while he tries to cut our pay

***

Living

- 'Success and happiness are the best defence against sour grapes.'

- 'Switch off the TV for a week and enjoy your life.'

- 'Racism - It can be subtle or blunt but it comes down to the same thing. I feel inferior to you so I will refer to your race in the hope that others who also feel inferior will support me.'

- 'Injustice destroys humanity'.

- 'Sometimes the only solution is laughter'.

- 'You can't run away from yourself'.

- 'Knowing others is wisdom - knowing yourself is enlightenment.' (Lao su.)

- 'None of us are as good or as bad as other people would portray us.'
- 'Do you own your things or do your things own you?' To find out switch off your phone, tv and computer for one day.

- 'Don't criticize those who can't help, just thank those who can.'

- 'Money cannot relieve the poverty in a cold heart.'

- 'Decency and fairness depend on leverage'.

- 'Take a day off'.

- 'It's easy to have integrity when you can afford it'.

- 'Beware false prophets, pollsters and journalists'

86

- 'In England those who retaliate to bad behaviour are considered to be guilty of '"making a fuss".'

- 'Physical chastisement in a moment of uncontrolled anger can quickly become excessive.'

- 'What a wonderful gift some people have, being omniscient after the fact.'

- 'Address the patterns of your own behaviour.'

- 'Sometimes there is no choice - sometimes trouble finds you.'

- 'Warriors defend those who can't defend themselves - fathers do the same.'

- 'Oh the irony!'

MARRIAGE/LOVE

---

[8] My mum, Hazel Anne Mance.

*

Noble Seats

Bluebird sings the harvest joy while cockerels dance their beat

Joyous crests display in smiles the wedding of our Mogul Prince

Sweet joining worlds and happy words connect two noble seats

The Arctic Queen so blond and fair awaits his courtly bow

While singing throng on shoulders high present the groom and host

What wonders lay before their feet through paths of new laid snow

A golden song of love, of peace anew - departure of old ghosts.

***

- 'Being a man means taking responsibility for others, protecting them, providing for them and setting a good example - for a long time.'

- 'If you are going to go over a waterfall you might as well swallow dive'.

- 'If you love to hate... you hate to love.'

- 'Crazy people make you crazy.'

- 'Good stuff happens too.'

- 'Sometimes people don't want the answer – they just want you to listen.'

Not Love You?

How could I not love you?
You from where all beauty
Is conceived in smiles
With expectations
Of new hope.
Future.

How could I not love you?
Without whom my life
Would be empty farce
Of toys and masks
Mother of life.
Creator.

How could I not love you?[9]

---

[9] Heather Joan Horsfall

'When you are wrong apologise but when you are right you are right. Just give hugs'

- 'Long term relationships are built on trust not love.'

- 'Family weddings are a maelstrom of conflicting emotions.'
- 'My wife knows me so well she argues with my thoughts.'

***

The Umbrella Sonnet

I wanted to change an umbrella

You thought I was changing the world

No longer a viable fellow

You scolded and made me feel cold

My words had shattered your vision

The change had taken your trust

To replace your new institution

With objects that water will rust

Now that your project is broken

The brolly will not be unfurled

Please take back the cruelty spoken

And see that my heart is not cold.

Or now in our unbroken silence

Will you leave our parasol rolled?

***

- 'Don't just buy your child a ball – play ball.'

- 'I'll never be rich but with my family I'll never be lonely – as a result - I'll always be rich.'

***

Women's Hair

Copper, corn, snow and wood cascade over round shoulders

To distract my thoughts with words that blind my mind

In shifting curls and changing shades created in His light

To cast a spell and shine on eyes that cannot turn away

From such beautiful creations.

***

Shoggy

If soldiers joined their battalions in Northern Ireland half way through tour they would be required to attend a week of Northern Ireland Training at Ballykinler. At the end of the said week each soldier was sent for one day with a unit other than his own. In 1975 I completed my week of training and was sent for a day on patrol with the Black Watch.

Bill my appointed patrol commander greeted me with 'Hellooo Robbie' and swapped my Parachute Regiment smock and Beret for a standard army combat jacket and a Black Watch Tam –o- shanty with a red hackle. 'Ye've got to look like us' said the corporal 'we can't have ye oot on the street wearin' that shite.'

As we left the camp he shouted up at a guard in the tower above the main gate. The towers were known as 'sangars'. They were built from concrete blocks and surrounded by wire netting that was supposed to be a protection against rockets. 'Hey Shoggy you keep yer eyes open up there son.' A metal grill slid back and for a moment a smiling camouflaged face appeared in the opening.' The reply wasn't translatable into modern English.

Our two-hour patrol was quiet until the muffled crump of an explosion in the distance interrupted our day. Bill checked in and was ordered to finish his patrol and return as arranged. When we eventually got back to camp we were confronted with the sight of Shoggy's Sangar reduced to rubble.

Bill asked one of the troops

'Oh hell. What happened to Shoggy'.

Oh that wee f***. He's in the nick the Sergeant Major locked him up.

'How' that?'

Well said the soldier the Sergeant-Major pulled him out of the rubble and said to him

'Hey Shoggy are ye alright son?

'Aye' says Shoggy 'aam fine'.

'Yer a lucky wee man Shoggy' says the Sargeant Major.

'Aye' says Shoggy 'If aa hadna been asleep I woulda bin kilt.'

Dusty Vermin

I knew a man called Dusty or something close to that

He had an awesome following cos he wore a special hat

His wife was fair and lovely with a wicked little smile

But Dusty thought her cheeky grin was shared with rank and file

He thought she was a princess and locked her in the house

And when he went to lands afar he told her not to grouse

When Dusty left on missions he sealed up all the keys

But Sally shouted though the door for help on hands and knees

Her cries were promptly answered and the door was broken in

And Sally ran to to spend some time with friendly kith and kin

When the war was over and Dusty returned home

He turned her face from light to dark because she chose to roam

Dusty was a hero - the media said a star

His stories were of courage, which a woman could not mar

But one dark night when all was still and lights were blinking dim

She took her kids and pets and clothes and ran away from him

The home she found was distant, a refuge from the storm

Where many other women could shelter safe and warm

One day the vermin's actions were cast o'er six long days

But those who knew him better would say that 'bullshit pays'.

***

- 'If you behave despicably you will be despised.'

- 'Much more is achieved when you don't mind who gets the credit.'

Growing Old

- 'Only drink in good company'. (again)

- 'Think, question, challenge, argue, consider and discuss. Ask for evidence, sense, reasons, meaning. Eliminate, belief, conjecture, opinion and most of all emotion. Avoid historical imperatives, bigots and extremists so that one day you will discover your own truth.'

- 'Sixty today. No matter how old you get there is always someone older who says "When you get to my age."

- 'PFB - Pause for breath'.

- 'If I believed what everyone else said I would be sitting in a hole somewhere feeling sorry for myself... I'm not!'

- 'It doesn't matter how much weight I lose - I still look fat!'

'No one wants to sit next to their grandpa at school'. (Graduation aged 59)

- 'Nine out of ten old people frown because they can't see you or can't hear you - the tenth one just doesn't like you.'

- 'The older one gets the madder the world seems.'

---

[10] Photo. Heather Horsfall

- 'Posting on Facebook is like panning for gold. It's worth it for those little bits of light in the mud.'

- 'Everyone wants to go to heaven but nobody wants to die'.

***

Dying

Don't cry because my life has bled

Or bawl about the days gone by

Or wail because my body's dead

With bitterness my soul shan't fly

Recall the days we shared in fun

Of girls and bars and lots of love.

Our youth when life did overrun

With dance and drink and carnal lust

Don't cry because I am no more

Old and lost by ancient lore

I'm dead and gone like those before

With faded scars of times of war

Remember that I had a life

Of pain and love with noble strife

With gain and loss, I cannot rue

My time with you - adieu, adieu.

***

- 'Those who know death every day enjoy all the blessings of life.'

Farewell

Lonely lover, only wife

Soft warm heart

Beats rhymes of life

Sooth and sing as I depart

Hold my face and kiss my tears

Within your warmth I softly lie

Your calming tones allay all fears

To make me peaceful as I die.

'God gets us all in the end.'

11

'NLTBGYD!'

---

11 Photo John Miller.

Previous publications by Robin Horsfall.

Unleash the Lioness. Robin Houseman (1992) Hodder and Stoughton. London

Fighting Scared. Robin Horsfall (2002). Wendell Nicolson. London

Printed in Great Britain
by Amazon

56992077R00061